Flames of Chelsea ~ 1908

Laura Thibodeau Jones

AuthorHouse™
1663 Liberty Drive
Bloomington, IN 47403
www.authorhouse.com
Phone: 1-800-839-8640

Published by AuthorHouse 8/26/2014

ISBN: 978-1-4969-3356-0 (sc)
ISBN: 978-1-4969-3357-7 (e)

Library of Congress Control Number: 2014914999

This book is a work of non-fiction. Unless otherwise noted, the author and the publisher make no explicit guarantees as to the accuracy of the information contained in this book and in some cases, names of people and places have been altered to protect their privacy.

Any people depicted in stock imagery provided by Thinkstock are models, and such images are being used for illustrative purposes only. Certain stock imagery © Thinkstock.

This book is printed on acid-free paper.

Because of the dynamic nature of the Internet, any web addresses or links contained in this book may have changed since publication and may no longer be valid. The views expressed in this work are solely those of the author and do not necessarily reflect the views of the publisher, and the publisher hereby disclaims any responsibility for them.

CONTENTS

This book is in honor of my Great Grandparents, August and Christina Reekast, my Grandmother, Ida Reekast Knoll and her seven siblings. Also, all the citizens of Chelsea, Massachusetts that endured heartache from this monster who ripped their lives apart...and for those poor souls, who lost their lives.

Special thanks to Aaron Schmidt, of the Boston Public Library, for bringing the images to my attention and for all your help.

To the unknown photographer, who's images fill most of the pages of this book...

Thank you for your photo history.

To Mom, who's strength and love, goes beyond my understanding.

To my Husband, for believing in me and loving me.

To my Dad, Sister and Brother...my heart aches for you, but somehow I feel your love lifting me up, every moment of everyday.

God Bless all of you.

April 18, 1936

I close my eyes and try to imagine my Great Grandfather on that day in April 1936.

A clear crisp spring day, when August Reekast dragged his double ender boat, 3 Sisters down the beach on King Cove in North Weymouth Massachusetts. The waves splashing the shore as his boat enters the water. He climbs aboard with the sun beaming on his face. He starts his long journey to the islands as he did so many times before. He rounds the corner to Fore River, with the view of Hull Gut in the distance. He rows with the strength of a twenty-six year old man, his arms feel strong, his heart full of love, as he enters the gut and rows past the beach he took his baby daughter Ida to fish, a life time ago. He continues until he reaches his determined destination. He becomes excited as he views the beautiful, Brewsters he loves so much... Oh how he longs to be home...he then views Calf Island, tears fill his eyes as he stares at her...it is as if he is looking into the past as the waves and sea air lull him back in time...

This is what I imagine my Great Grandfather's last day to be...going home to the islands.

August Reekast closed his eyes for the last time on this day in April 1936.

My Great Grandmother, Christina Reekast, joined him, many years later...

August 29, 1951.

They both lived an extremely difficult life...but they survived with pride and love...together.

INTRODUCTION
The Beginning of the End

The Year is 1908, Chelsea Massachusetts, Palm Sunday, April 12, the fire bells rang...a split second in time was all it took for my great grandparents, August and Christina Reekast and their eight children...August Jr, Nettie, Annie, John, Lillian, Lena, Ida and Teddy to lose everything.

A Massive fire ripped through the City of Chelsea, Massachusetts, the flames, so intense, reports of the fires glow was seen one hundred twenty miles away off the coast line of Maine. This monster was reported to have taken the lives of eighty-seven and left approximately eighteen thousand homeless. From that moment on, life as the Reekast family~(My family) ~ and all the citizens of Chelsea, would never be the same.

After battling the fire, turning to the only life he knew. August Reekast rowed his family over nine miles to safety out of the flames and flying ashes of the Chelsea fire, to the Boston Harbor Islands, where they spent years rebuilding their lives living in shacks built out of old drift wood from shipwrecks.

Today, in April 2014, the winds are howling from this early Nor'easter, the rain pounding on my windows, the ocean waves slapping on our deck in fury, my mind rushes to my family on Middle and Great Brewster Island in Boston Harbor. It was April in 1908, when they came to live in a shack on Middle Brewster Island and later Great Brewster. I cannot imagine what they were doing on a day like today, possibly huddled up on the floor, or the children laying in their make shift cots in fear as their parents battle to keep them and their cottage / hut safe.

I realize, it was 106 years ago and there is absolutely no comparison I can make, not even camping in the grimmest of conditions would rank in measurement to what my family endured...For that matter...the shock of being in one of, if not the most massive fires of it's time.

I do know, most of us do not know the pain of being homeless...or the desperation of how to feed and keep our children warm, but most importantly, out of harms way. Not only did my family battle the elements, but the would be thieves that prayed upon the weak. What August Reekast, my great grandfather, must have gone through at the time, trying to protect his family at all cost, as the provider ~ protector. Having the decision of making his boys into men years before their time...I often get a sick feeling inside, trying to picture my great grandmother, Christina Reekast, a Mom of eight babies, ages ranging from three to thirteen, keeping a brave face for them, I am sure with tears in her eyes, telling them everything would be 'all right...knowing', they would never go home again.

CHAPTER I
Chelsea Massachusetts ~ Time Line

The history of Chelsea Massachusetts, is quite impressive, located on a peninsula in Boston Harbor and dating as far back as the1600s...the Massachusetts Indians owned the land and lived in as many as twenty villages in and around Boston Harbor. In 1624, the English influence began in Chelsea, when an Englishman named Samuel Maverick settled in what was then called Winnisimmet ~ 'meaning...' "good spring nearby." and owned by the children of Nanepashemet...Sagamore John (Wonohaquaham), Sagamore James (Montowompate) and Sagamore George (Wenepoykin). Samuel Maverick and his brother, Elias, along with Robert Arnold and William Stitson were named as the earlier settlers in Winnisimmet.

Winnisimmet was composed of, Chelsea, Winthrop, Revere and Saugus. Samuel Maverick built the first house in 1625...said to be a fortified (fortify...to protect or strengthen against attack) house near the waters' edge and the Chelsea bridge. This was the first house in the Massachusetts Bay Colony and was reported to have still been standing in 1660s, however, one account rumored, as late as the revolution. Maverick acquired Winnisimmet through trades with the Indians, which was documented as some five thousand acres of land.

Samuel Maverick (Mavericke) married the widow of David Thompson in 1628 owner of (now) Thompson and Noodle Island (now Logan Airport). Upon Thompson's death, his wife Amias and only son, inherited all of his possessions.

Winnisimmet was sold to Governor Richard Birmingham by Maverick, keeping only, his house and farm land ...Birmingham became Governor of the Massachusetts Bay Colony...he also built a home, which he named The Carey House...The Carey House still stands today.

In 1738, Winnisimmet was separated from Boston, and incorporated as the town of Chelsea.

The population in Winnisimmet ~ Chelsea, also known as Rumny Marsh was as follows;

1765 ~ 462
1790 ~ 472
1800 ~ 849
1830 ~ 770

In 1831, eight people (individuals) bought the land and the ferry franchise, by 1833, the population began to increase as the Winnisimmet Company was incorporated. By 1840, the population grew to 2,182...1846...the towns were separated as, North Chelsea and Winthrop. The population in 1850 was 6,151, 1860, 13,395, and by 1865, 14,403. In 1857, it was incorporated a city.

The earlier settlers noted Chelsea to be a "Very sweet place...for situation, and stands very commodiously." The Boston Harbor Islands were known for keeping off the winds and sea, tempering the winters and water of the bay mitigating the heat of the summer. Therefore, a very desirable place to settle.

CHAPTER 2
Before the Fire

Life before the fire in Chelsea Massachusetts, seemed to be a place full of hope, even in this historically over populated small city. The businesses and trading industries of rubber and rags, shoes and stores upon stores was seemly booming. Yes, no doubt, there were struggles, but life for face value seemed normal.

Chelsea, a city established in the early 1600s, by all accounts was new and upcoming in the mid-1800s. The names of her first settlers were memorialized in the center square and in streets names.

Old landmark homes were still in tack and seemed to be honored for it.

By the late 1800s Chelsea had a diverse mix of citizens. Immigrants from all walks of life, settled here and were attempting to build the American dream. It has been said the "upper class" wealthy names in the city, began to leave this increasingly desired sea side village, they were not willing to except the changes to their once loved home. The city was nicknamed "dead as Chelsea." Citizens were determined to change the rumors, as Chelsea at one time had a colorful and rich reputation of well-to-dos, from lawyers, actors, politicians, bankers, writers and the list goes on.

Before the fire

The turn of the century was a colorful world with light hearted love and respect. The women wore stunning gowns, gloves and hats...full body attire on the sandy beaches. The men dressed in suits with gloves and top hats and they too were fully dressed on a hot sunny day on the beaches and in the waters. Their dreams were grand, full of hopes of a new world.

Looking into the past, I may be romanticizing, but, it appeared to be a time when families, friends and neighbors enjoyed each other. They did not have what we do today, but somehow they had more.

I guess it just seemed to be a time of hope and somehow, a time of innocents. Everything, from homes to streets and town landmarks were all new, brilliant colors and smells of blooming flowers. With no TV or radio to occupy their time, they sat around for family readings, or took long walks after a hard day. There were gatherings in the center of town and parades for all occasions. Beaches were filled with men, women and children lying around listening to big bands. They would travel to near by towns to newly built amusement parks or would canoe on the Charles River.

The next few pages are of old Chelsea and Chelsea in 1908 before the fire ~ bit of their past...from the beginning of Chelsea to the destruction...

Chelsea, Mass. Ye Old Pratt House, Built 1660.

OLD PRATT HOUSE, BUILT 1660, OLDEST HOUSE IN CHELSEA, MASS.

2226.

The Patten's are all right so said. He heard from them yesterday Lizzie

9

OLD CAREY MANSION IN WINTER, CHELSEA, MASS.

:227.

PHOTO BY SLADE.

CHELSEA, ... 190

First Primary School in Chelsea.

JOHN F. GILMAN, CHELSEA, MASS.

10

Chelsea Common and Washington Square.

575—
Chelsea
Water
Department,
Chelsea,
Mass.

got
your
letter to
day I
am well
and hope
you are
as usual
Prie
haint
very
well
love
Lena

574—
Frost
Hospital,
Chelsea,
Mass.

13

Canoeing on the Charles.

How would you like to be here.

July 17, 1905

W. H. Tupper

Published by The Metropolitan News Co., Boston.

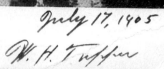
Listening to the Band, Nantasket Beach, Mass.

STATE BATH HOUSE
REVERE BEACH

Owens Bros., Publishers, 19 Washington St , Boston.

ON THE BOARD WALK, LOOKING TOWARDS JAPAN, WONDERLAND, REVERE BEACH, MASS.

SER. 780-1. BATHERS AT REVERE BEACH, MASS. *Love from Alma*

A Scamper on the Beach

Nantasket Beach, Mass.

FERRYBOAT "CITY OF CHELSEA", CHELSEA, MASS.

2210.

PHOTO BY SLADE.

Thomas Williams established the first Ferry, May 18, 1631, between Winnettsem and Charlton and "thence to Boston." This was the first ferry established in the United States... over time... Chelsea Massachusetts had their own ferry ~ City of Chelsea.

CHAPTER 3
April Showers

The day started like any other day in the city of Chelsea Massachusetts. A beautiful Sunday morning April 12, 1908. The weather was cool with increasingly high winds coming off the ocean ~ men, women, and children went about their normal activities to ready themselves for Palm Sunday Mass.

Never could any citizen of Chelsea Massachusetts, imagine there was a monster brewing, lurking in wait for the exact moment to strike. And strike it did.

The fire bells rang roughly before eleven...many members were leaving St. Rose Church, while some were still inside. There seem to be no immediate panic among the general public, but soon concern grew, as off in the distance dark smoke filled the sky.

The fire started just off Summer Street, close to the Everett line at the Boston Blacking Company. The Boston Blacking Company, made shoe's and adhesives and was located on West Third Street. It was reported the roof caught fire from a burning pile of rags, which began in the dump site in the rear of the building. Full of oil, the building ignited into an uncontrollable scene. The flames were first reported approximately at ten forty-four a.m., and with wind gusts of forty to fifty miles per hour, the sparks went flying to the center of the city.

As a precaution, a second alarm was sounded, ordered by Fire Chief Spencer upon his arrival at the scene. The first fire was contained, however, soon after, the site of another building was inflamed. Two blocks away, T. Lewitzky & son's, three story rag shop was engulfed. This was the end all to the city as they knew it...building by building...the fire could not be contained. The factory district was full of companies such as; Chapin & Sawdin a tar paper factory, which caught on fire and was reported, the flames were so intense due to the heat of the tar paper, it drove the firefighters back.

Old landmark homes had no defense, the fire ripped through the streets one by one burning everything in it's wake. From Maple Street to Summer, West Third to Elm to Arlington, these flames showed no mercy...Spruce Street and Everett Avenue...all was lost. The flames were leaping over buildings...almost looking back with vengeance.

Only moments before, these once beautiful street's full of rich vibrant homes and beautiful trees were nothing but burning ashes.

By all accounts... Chelsea residents believed the fire would be contained...not until the fire past Arlington Street did panic ensue...men and women trying to save any of their belongings they could carry. Mayhem broke out with people refusing to leave their homes...Grabbing old mattresses to protect themselves from the heat and fury of the flames, only for them to catch fire which created more damage, as pieces of the material flew throughout the streets.

Desperate attempts to save their homes, quickly changed to saving their children. Women and children pleading for help from anyone that could hear them or for that matter anyone that could see them. Reports of ... bloodcurdling screams could be heard in the distance. Through the flames and the smoke and flying ashes...most families got separated, losing not only there husbands and wives, but their babies.

Many animals from dogs, cats, horses and hens were found burned to death. One report stated, they could hear the hoofs of the horses scrambling in the pea thick smoke.

Sheer desperation was seen on the faces of not only the residents of Chelsea, but in the faces of the fire men. Fighting a fire more intense then ever before, fire engines called streamers were melting in front of them...they could not contain this monster with the gusts of winds of over fifty miles per hour, even with hundreds of fire fighters from surrounding cities and towns on the scene...the elements were against them. The fire fighters heroic and exhausting efforts, during what began as a two alarm fire and ended in a monstrous conflagration, did not go unnoticed...even with the knowledge of their own families and property in danger, they did not leave their post...what was left of this city was due to their unwavering determination, strong sense of duty...and heavy hearts.

IN THE HEART OF THE CHELSEA FIRE.

COPYRIGHT 1908
THOMAS E PENARD

BELLINGHAM HILL
CHELSEA FIRE, APRIL 12, 1908--VIEW FROM EVERETT

May 15-08.   START OF FIRE
This was only the start
should have seen it later

21

Boston's Largest Engine abandoned and destroyed at the Chelsea Fire April 12, 1908.

RUINS OF ENGINE NO. 1 OF LYNN CHELSEA

22

In this image, you can see the fury of the gusting winds, blowing smoke around Washington Avenue.

Fire chief, H.A. Spencer was a resident of Chelsea Massachusetts since the age of six. He was a veteran in the fire department for over thirty years, before being promoted to Chief in 1889. His record was impeccable as chief, with the lowest total losses in any year and very well respected by all. Noted to be one of the most popular officials. A former Navy man, he was also a member of the Knight Templar Mason, star of Bethlehem Lodge and the Theodore Winthrop post.

Looking down Shawmut Street and the corner of Maverick, both corners of the Fire.

The above photo is the view of the fire from Marine Hill.

The fire was so intense, the smoke was seen miles away. There were many reports of fire, especially from Boston... This is the Arlington Street Church, located at the corner of the Public Garden's in Boston.

Ruins at Everett, Wa.

Not even the water front was safe from the wrath of the flames. Reported: Two schooners, docked near the Oil Co., went up in flames, however, caught in time, the damages was minimal. Feared, the shipyard would also be at risk, fire boats on the harbor were despatched...with no reports of loss...what potentially could have been a disaster, was quickly contained.

CHAPTER 4
Reports of Fire and Panic in the Streets

The Youth's Companion ~ New England Editions, April 30, 1908

On the front page of the paper are two compelling photo's of a city burnt. The Ruins of the City Hall and a view of Washington Avenue, south from the Chelsea railroad station... The article was listed on page 214 under Current Events and read in part:

A great fire in Chelsea, Massachusetts destroyed about one-third of the city. It appeared to be a trifling (insignificant) blaze until a strong gale carried the flames and destroyed an area of two miles and a half long and a mile wide. About ten thousand homeless and ten persons lost their lives and others reported missing. The fire raged on for twelve hours or until it was brought under control.

It destroyed building as follows:

- City Hall
- Six school houses
- The Public Library
- Blocks of businesses and factories
- Eleven churches
- Two hospitals

Fort Wayne Weekly Journal - Gazette ~ April 13, 1908

FIRE SWEEPS MORE THAN A SQUARE MILE: Loss reaches $9,000,000

Fanned by furious gale, the flames licked up:

Churches, the library, schools, great manufactories and City Hall.

Disaster at glance: The fire was beyond control even with a dozen city departments called to assist. An apparently insignificant fire started among rags on a dumps site, but was fanned by a northwest gale into a conflagration which obliterated nearly one-third of the city.

Five hundred dwelling houses and public buildings were destroyed. Fifteen hundred families driven from their habitations, while ten thousand left homeless...two are known to be reported lost. The article goes on to say: at a late hour tonight, it was reported another had perished. A women was said to have shot herself in a panic apparently so distraught over not being able to save her property...at least one hundred are reported injured, at this time an accurate estimate of loss is near impossible.

Boston April 12...this newspaper referred to the Chelsea Fire as, "The Greatest Fire that has scoured any part of the metropolitan district in ten years." Starting at ten forty a.m. this fire was not under control until at least seven o'clock p.m. and not withstanding half of the Boston Fire Departments strength and streamers from a dozen other cities and towns came to the aide of the Chelsea brigade. Until seven, reports of fifteen hundred families homeless and at this time, two or three reports of fatalities.

The fire was reported to have originated in the rear of the Boston Blacking Company, located on West Third Street. With gales of up to sixty miles an hour...it sent sparks of embers and carried burning shingles throughout the streets. Starting in extreme southwest section of the city, the fire cut a path to the end of the southeastern part of the city, which boarders the Chelsea creek.

...partment in Action.
Chelsea, Mass. April 12th, 1908.

The description from these photo's read as follows:

No.2 Engine

1-Capt. J.F. Hutchins 2~F.J Mealey 3~T.F. Kelley 4~A.H. Stitt

Tel. Alarm from Chelsea, received at 4:56 PM. Engine 2 and Hose 2 left quarters at 4:59 PM. Returned at 11:30 PM. Sunday, April 12, 1908.

No. 2 Brookline = Hose

1 ~ Capt. F. W. Brachett 2~P. A. Mealey 3~M. J. Nolan 4~E. J. Forbes
5~ J. W. Kelley

Engine 5 at Chelsea Sept. 21-08

Many calls and cries were reported from the surrounding communities with reports of tragedy.

One man found dead and burned to death, while attempting to cross the bridge to East Boston. Reports of a couple, who committed suicide...a women died on the way to the hospital in an ambulance, while it was reported, another shot herself in a panic, not being able to save her property.

HAND MADE POSTAL CO.
WAKEFIELD, MASS.

B and A R. R. Bridge and Old Chelsea Bridge from East Boston.

Reports of even more danger lurking...Telephone and telegraph wires dangling in the streets and all communications were cut off...The City was in total darkness with homeless huddled around the smoldering ruins for light and warmth.

There was Panic in the streets and many fled to Boston. The thousands who did not flee, were camped in the streets and in vacant lots. All was lost to those individuals and were left homeless and penniless. Only a few homes of the rich were destroyed.

Tents created to shelter refuges and Militia

A child was found crying in the street...said to be a young girl about the age of twelve. She was sitting right in the middle of Bellingham Street, a few feet from the square. Frighten, alone and tired, she held in her arms a bible. A reporter that was running up Bellingham Hill, asked if he could help her and she told him the bible was heavy and she could no longer carry it, but wanted to keep it safe from being burned. At the same time, a wagon full of items was passing by, the reporter asked the driver if he would take the bible and keep it safe...the driver agreed he would until the time the family claimed it. The little girl was at ease and began to follow behind the wagon.

Picture below of Bellingham Hill.

A piano solo midst the ruins.

The spirit of Chelsea Massachusetts and her people can be seen in the gentle men in the above image. Trying to save their piano, they covered it with a cloth. When the cloth caught fire, they realized they were no match for the fire, opened the lid and played, ***"There'll be a hot time in the old town to-night."***

CHAPTER 5
Homeless ~ but Not alone

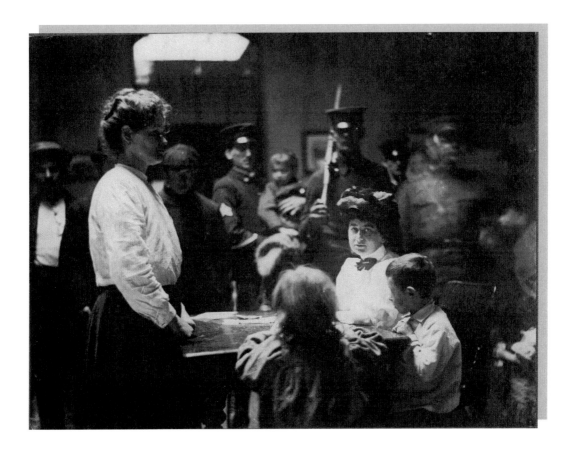

Families spending the night at the Chelsea High School

Chelsea high school was dedicated the headquarters for the Chelsea Relief Committee. The committee was organized in the early evening of the fire, their main priority was to direct the homeless to housing...Churches... etc. In the hours to follow, they organized an information center to report and locate missing family members. Also, a food counter was started in the basement, where loads of food and supplies were delivered.

Other sites were also opened: The Salvation Army Barracks in Chelsea Square, Saint Luke's Parsonage, Scenic Temple, The Cary Avenue Methodist Church, First Congregation Church, and the Soldier's Home.

Scene at the high school ~ the morning after the fire.

Delivering mattresses and supplies for the refugees at the Chelsea High School.

Unloading supplies at the High School ~ Relief Headquarters

Collecting food and clothing in the West End of Boston Massachusetts for the fire sufferers...

In Chelsea, at the relief centers, the amount of food that was distributed in one day was documented as ~ 400 gallons of milk, 1,000 dozen of eggs, 600 gallons of coffee, 175 cases of canned meat and soup, 1,200 cans of condensed milk and 500 pound of sugar.

In addition, clothing items were donated...2,600 undergarments for children, women and men, over 100 shoes, mattresses and pillows were reported to be 500 each and approximately 1000 blankets were collected.

Young fire sufferers, coming successfully out of the high school relief line.

Entertaining the homeless children with games at the South Armory.

Through all the panic and mayhem, volunteers try to keep the children's minds away from fear...

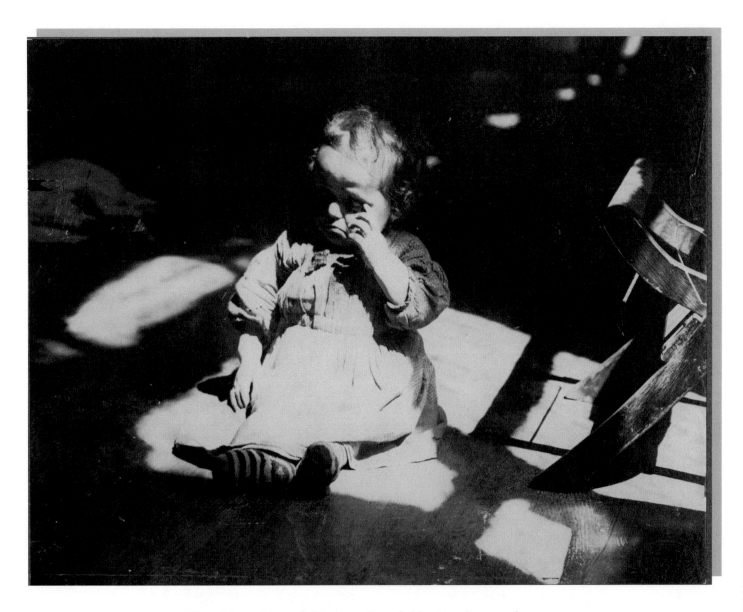

The above photo of this homeless child ~ breaks your heart.

St. Rose Catholic Church, Chelsea, Mass.

St. Rose Church, destroyed by the fire.

Members of St. Rose Church attending Mass at the old parish house...
Saint Rose Church was destroyed in the fire.

As I look at this image, looking into the crowd, I wonder if my family was in attendance this day...over one hundred years later, there is such pain in my heart for all of these people...as if it just happened yesterday.

Chapter 6
Militia Called

Militia troops were called in to Chelsea Massachusetts and by ten p.m. Martial Law was in effect.

Stations were established in all sections of the city. The initial orders were as follows:

1. Police Headquarters will be the battalion headquarters until further notice.

2. No one will be allowed to carry away or disturb any private property from the ruins without a signed permit signed by the proper authorities. Officers will be held accountable for the district.

   Enlisted men will not trespass upon private property.

3. Officers and men will assist the city government members and police.

4. Instructed Lieutenant Williams of the Eighth infantry to inspect sanitary conditions.

5. Captain Whitney of the Fifth Infantry to inspect and report the safety of the burnt district.

Residents who left the city found it difficult to gain entrance back to Chelsea. Passes were issued...there were three-forms and had specific purposes...each pass was color coded...

Blue ~ admitted to the lines which was taken up.

White ~ allowed the bearer to search among the ruins

A special permit ... Permit to enter upon Property ~ this was good for one day only.

(Name of holder) has permission to enter *(number)* street, previously occupied by him, to examine premises, open safe and remove property belonging to him...

Between the hours of 8am and 5pm...April ..., 1908.

Soldiers keeping crowd at a safe distance.

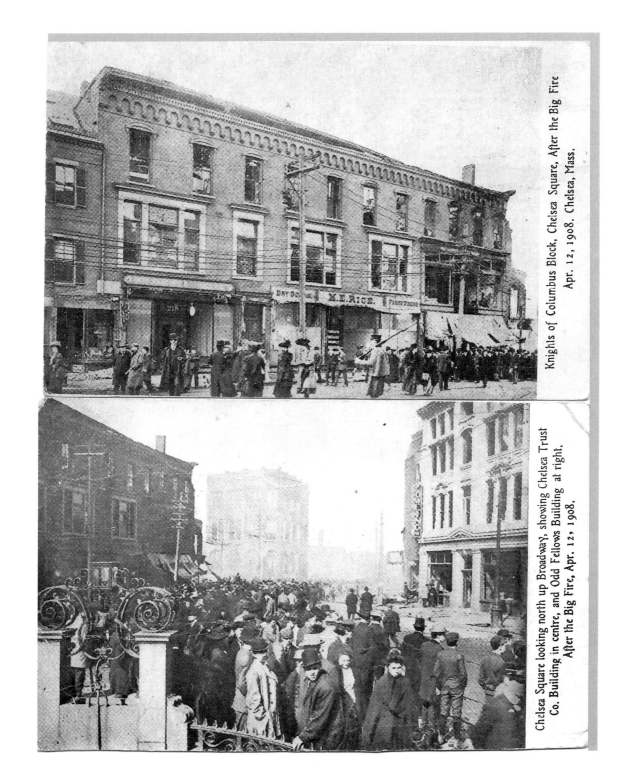

Knights of Columbus Block, Chelsea Square, After the Big Fire Apr. 12, 1908. Chelsea, Mass.

Chelsea Square looking north up Broadway, showing Chelsea Trust Co. Building in centre, and Odd Fellows Building at right. After the Big Fire, Apr. 12, 1908.

Chelsea Merchant and wife, opening safe...Store on Broadway.

Searching the ruins

Burned out residents of Park Street ~ trying to save some of their household goods.

CHAPTER 7
Days that followed

Two little girls, guarding a few things saved from their home.

Household effects stored in Chelsea Square.

Burned out residents on Pear Street.

Hauling household goods to a place of safety

Woman standing at the ruins of her home ~ the morning after the fire.

All that was saved

Clean away on Chestnut Street.

Relaying the car tracks on Broadway.

Early workers assemble at burnt district.

Gathering at the ruins

Jesse Gould & Son before being destroyed in the massive fire.

A resumption of business (Jesse Gould & Son) - 195 Washington Ave.

Food line for the fire victims ~ Chelsea, Massachusetts.

Supplies for the Passover, distributed by ~Young Men's Hebrew Association.

Refuges supplied with clothing by Senator Klonahan in Charlestown.

A private relief party inquiring...Where best to go?

There was No where for the citizen's of Chelsea to go...homeless and penniless.

Temporary building erected by the Telephone Company for an exchange.

Sadly, if the citizens of Chelsea had not gone through enough, there were predators lurking. Some who would stand in the food and clothing lines representing themselves as Chelsea victims. It was reported, they then took the articles only to sell them in Boston and in nearby towns. Thank goodness, there were only a few, the authorities were alerted, which prompted yet another pass they needed to apply for.

Volunteers from everywhere flooded the streets of Chelsea. They did not look upon them as lost souls, but with admiration. The commonwealth rallied around this city and will not be remembered by the few, but by the droves of volunteers that work tirelessly to help...in food lines and clothing lines, taking in the homeless or caring for their children, working round the clock with the dying and wounded, and the caring for the helpless animals. Most importantly...the city will be remembered for the undying Spirit of her people.

In the days to come...the cleanup. The city began the clean away two days after the monster struck.

The 1908 fire will be remembered as one of the most devastating fires of it's time. The memory of the strength and pride from the good people of Chelsea should impress all that read about them and their losses, but most importantly the determination...unwillingness to lay down in defeat.

Great Grandfather, August Reekast on his boat "3 Sisters"

Above is a picture of my Great Grandmother, Christina Reekast on Great Brewster...this is years after the 1908 fire.

View from Middle Brewster ~ early 1900s

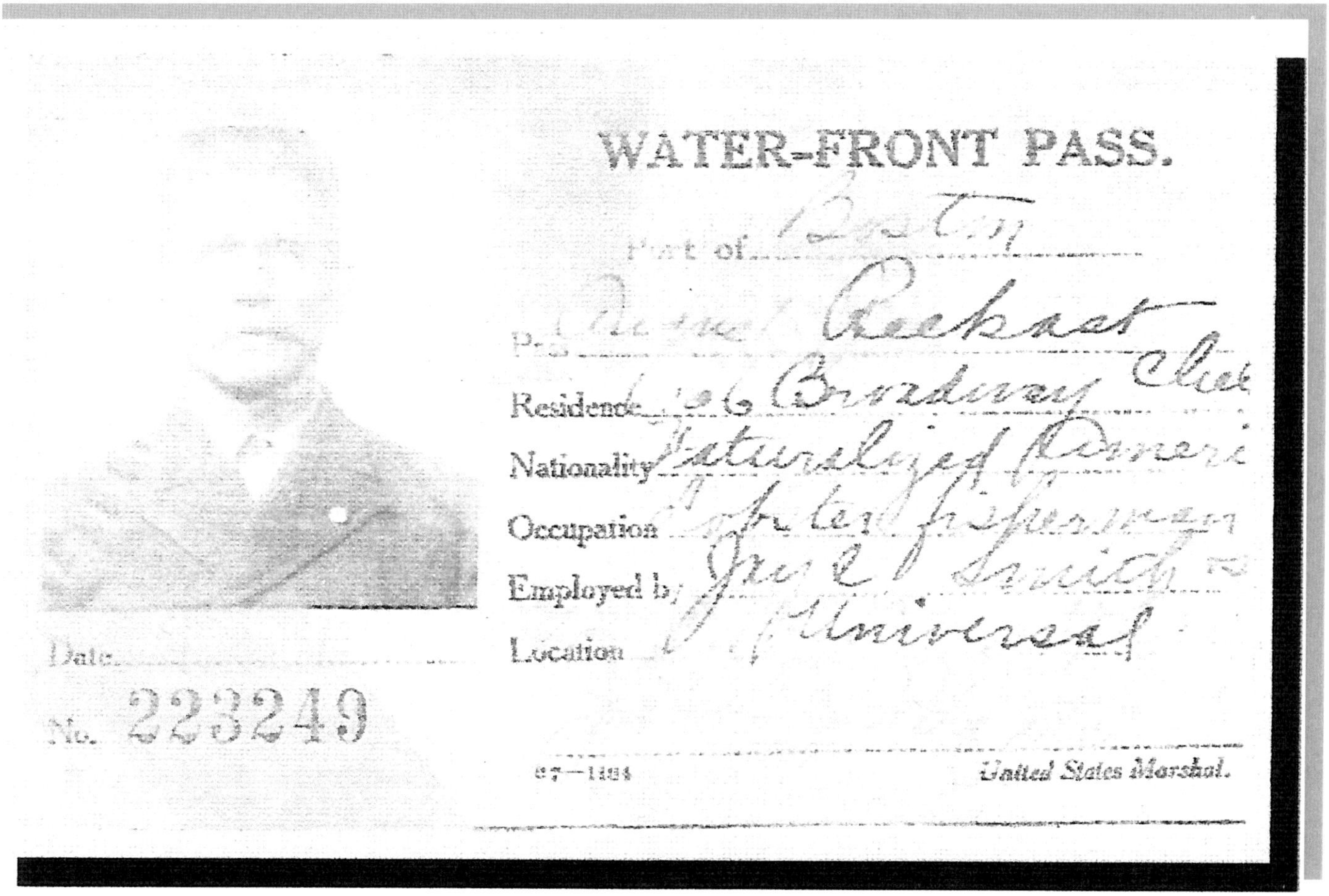

WATER-FRONT PASS.

Port of _Boston_

P. _Arthur Reekast_

Residence _106 Broadway Chel._

Nationality _Naturalized Ameri_

Occupation _lobster fisherman_

Employed by _Jry E. Smith —_

Location _Universal_

Date _____

No. 223249

87—1898

United States Marshal.

In 1917, the Reekast family moved back to Chelsea Massachusetts, living at 106 Broadway...Never truly leaving the islands, they continued to live seasonally (April - October) on Brewster and Calf Islands.

I wonder what life would have held for the Reekast family and all the families of Chelsea...if it were not for this tragic event in time. An event that no doubt will in years to come be noted as a fire out of a horror scene...a fire larger than one could possibly imagine.

My family went on to rebuild their life living on an island that was desolate...no running water, no appliances... not one luxury item that time could afford, not even a home to call their own. August and Christina Reekast, went from a very comfortable life...to nothing, they paved the way for generations to come living on the islands of Boston Harbor and in doing so, created yet another historical event in time. They spent nearly a decade on Great Brewster Island, before moving to East Boston, then back to Chelsea in 1917.

August Reekast

THE CITY HALL

THE CARNEGIE LIBRARY

It took nearly two years for the city to rise up again. The recovery was reported to be one of the most progressive communities of Massachusetts. With the fire destroying most the public buildings...almost the entire business section was lost. Schools, Churches and homes were totally gone...Approximately eighteen thousand were left homeless...damages of over fifteen million dollars were reported. But this did not stop them. Remarkably, by 1910, a new and improved Chelsea was reborn.

My family was among the thousands that lost everything in the massive fire. The only item we know of, that was saved, (except maybe for some smoke filled clothing), is the picture below. It is a picture of my Great Uncle Teddy before the Chelsea fire. He was my Grandmother's (Ida Knoll) youngest brother ~ Ted Lawrence Reekast.

At a very young age tragedy found him and sadly, followed him. Years later, after leaving the Islands of Boston Harbor, Teddy went to work on an oil tanker, The Cities Service Denver. On March 26, 1941, the Denver was blown up at sea, off the Carolinas. The New York Times described the Denver as a flaming mass, killing twenty crew members, with twenty-one survivors.

There was a search for additional survivors by the Coast Guard and seaplanes, but found only empty life boats. There was no explanation given for the explosion, except is was mysterious.

Great Uncle Teddy was listed among the missing...as Lawrence T. Reekast of East Weymouth Mass. Teddy Reekast, lost his life at the young age of thirty-six.

Great Uncle Teddy

In closing...I would like to thank my Great Grandparents for being so strong, and for keeping our family together.

Sources

The Boston Public Library ~ Imagining Department

The Unknown Photographer ~ 1908.

Boston Harbor ~ Illustrated - Published by The Photo Electrotype Co. 1879

The City of Chelsea Massachusetts ~Illustrated~The Gazette~Published 1898.

A Historical Discourse, delivered at Chelsea, Mass, September 20, 1866...at the Twenty-fifth Anniversary of the Winnisimmet Congregational Church. By Isaac P. Langworthy, First Pastor...Chelsea, 1866.

The Burning of Chelsea...By: Walter Merriam Pratt~First Published in Boston, Massachusetts ~1908.

Newspaper.com

Chicago Daily Tribune ~ Monday, April 13, 1908.

The Wall Street Journal ~Tuesday, April, 14, 1908.

FT. Wayne Weekly Journal Gazette ~ Thursday, April 16, 1908.

The Washington Post ~ Monday, April 13, 1908.

The Youth's Companion ~New England Edition~ April 30, 1908.

The Youth's Companion ~ New England Edition~ November 10, 1910.

New York Times ~ March 26, 1941.

Printed in the United States
By Bookmasters